Sliver of Change

poems by

Marianne Brems

Finishing Line Press
Georgetown, Kentucky

Sliver of Change

For Joan

Copyright © 2020 by Marianne Brems
ISBN 978-1-64662-344-0 First Edition
All rights reserved under International and Pan-American Copyright Conventions. No part of this book may be reproduced in any manner whatsoever without written permission from the publisher, except in the case of brief quotations embodied in critical articles and reviews.

ACKNOWLEDGMENTS

"Sliver of Change" appeared in *Voice of Eve*, March 2019
"No Food by Mouth" appeared in *Thimble*, March 2019
"Authentically Anonymous" appeared in *Foliate Literary Magazine*, September 2018
"Reunion" appeared in *Avatar Review*, August 2019
"Dancing Fountain" appeared in *Nightingale & Sparrow*, May 2019
"Bright Boy" appeared in the *Pangolin Review,* May 2019
"Emptier than Empty" appeared in *Avatar Review*, August 2019
"Pfeiffer Canyon Bridge" appeared in *Mused*, Winter 2018
"Bicycle Chain" appeared in the *Pangolin Review*, September 2018
"We Can't Replant" appeared in *Scarlet Leaf Review*, December 2019
"The San Gabriel Aquaduct" appeared in *Mused*, Spring 2018
"Banana Spots" and "A Piano Falls" appeared in *Academy of the Heart and Mind*, January 2019

Publisher: Leah Huete de Maines
Editor: Christen Kincaid
Cover Art: Michael Jastremski
Author Photo: Joan Bresnan
Cover Design: Elizabeth Maines McCleavy

Order online: www.finishinglinepress.com
also available on amazon.com

Author inquiries and mail orders:
Finishing Line Press
P. O. Box 1626
Georgetown, Kentucky 40324
U. S. A.

Table of Contents

Introduction
Sliver of Change 1
No Food by Mouth 3
Authentically Anonymous 4
Golden Gate Morning 6
Ashes in the Lake 7
Reunion 8
Dancing Fountain 9
Sleep 10
Oatmeal Adventure 11
Bright Boy 12
Murky Sunlight 13
A Piano Falls 14
Moving Day 15
Spectator 16
Emptier than Empty 17
Night Siren 18
Pfeiffer Canyon Bridge 19
Tight Braids 20
Bicycle Chain 21
We Can't Replant 22
The San Gabriel Aquaduct 23
Politeness 24
Banana Spots 25
Lunar Majesty 26

Introduction

Transformations, small ones, big ones, frightening ones, peaceful ones occur at every moment. Each morning things are never exactly the same as the day before. Transformations continually trace the spiritual journey from one place to another. To comprehend then point to the relationship between one moment and the next is the work of the author who ornaments our brains.

Sliver of Change

Parents deliver malleable children
into the hands of teachers
who lead them through long hallways
papered with pictures of the presidents,
flags from around the world,
and personal experiences
recorded in the Tree Ring Project,
and lined with rows of backpacks
decorated with kittens,
Spiderman,
jack-o-lanterns,
princesses,
holding pencils,
bananas,
unfinished worksheets,
forgotten permission slips.

At the bell,
they catapult onto the playground,
liberated voices penetrating
the open air
as their small bodies leap and jerk,
twist and run,
and mature just a sliver
inside twenty minutes
before conforming in rows
by classroom number,
their furious energy soon confined
between four walls
to messy splendors
constructed with
butcher paper, paste, and paint.

As paint dries,
they put back supplies
learn multiplication tables,
read stories about wild things
each molding them a tiny fraction
before returning them
respectfully
to waiting parents.

No Food by Mouth

I carry into the hospital waiting area
the nameless constriction of my mourning.
Boxes of tissue wait on horizontal surfaces.
Every voice too loud.
Every noise amplified.

My mother hiked the Sierras into her 80s.
Played tennis until she was 90.
Now at 97 she lies with a fever of 102,
a needle in her arm,
little awareness of any of it.

Fellow strangers wait near me.
No reason to speak.
One offers me a cup of water.
My mother was here just
three months ago I say.

We talk about the mothers
we will have for a little longer,
the bond they cinched in our hearts,
their travel down love's unpaved roads,
their departure from cognition,
the tangling of their feathers
against their will
in the chain-links of aging.

A nurse calls me.
I leave this better-known stranger
to hear what I already know.
Aspiration pneumonia the verdict.
No food by mouth the prescription.

As the fever shrinks,
my common sense grows.
ThickenUp and half-inch pieces
will have to do
for the next small forever.

Authentically Anonymous

In the time it takes to snap a twig,
your character disappears.
The airport doors,
and there are many,
gape
then swallow you whole
as you consult your watch
and search through artificial light
for check-in.

Cheerful ambassadors in uniforms
who mask fatigue with pasted smiles
glance at your ticket,
checking for the text
that validates your existence
before they scribble in red
and wave you on to the next bottleneck.

Long lines.
Please Wait says the entry flap
that collides with your stomach.
Travelers hurry to empty their lives
into gray plastic rectangles
resisting separation.
Belts off,
shoes in the bin,
data filled laptops naked.
Dingy trays
touched by millions
rumble away
through rubber strips
into a dark tunnel
with most of what's left of you.
Then re-emerge minus nail scissors
into the intrusive confusion
of reunification.

Authenticated by security,
only the numbers matter.
Your gate
Your flight
Your boarding time
Your group
Your row

Your exhausted mass
at last spills
into your numbered seat.
Endless layers all around
confine other masses,
necks crook'd,
eyes glazed,
staring absently
at tiny glowing screens.

Golden Gate Morning

Fog spills over the ridge like a cauldron.
Thick and soft as goose feathers,
swaddling a bridge
not ready to rise from sleep
beneath its hidden towers.
The majestic turned docile
inside a shroud of gray.

But within seconds,
like an apology for obstruction,
the north tower leaps through this curtain
in a sudden blaze of crimson
piercing the lucid azure sky.
Persistent wisps of fog
timidly seep over the ridge
but can no longer contain
a paramount cool sunlight.

Ashes in the Lake

As I slowly drop my mother's ashes
into the icy lake
she loved to walk around,
they cling near the surface
in a gray cotton cloud,
once hands reaching
with the urgency of love,
reluctant to spread
and allow the water
to dissipate her memory.

Reunion

In the swarm of arrivals
at the international terminal
an anxious welcomer perches
under oversized monitors,
her two young children
chasing one another,
tugging at each other's arms,
as anonymous depleted passengers
with luggage carts piled high
stream from a gaping linoleum hallway.

She watches clutching for relief
as others lean consummate
into the waiting arms of loved ones
then whisk themselves off
folded into easy gestures of familiarity.

With each departing cluster,
nagging emptiness grows,
filling her eyes
that settle without recognition
on the faces of every emerging traveler.

The minutes drip by.
Her children now bump in boredom
against her,
the face of their auntie dimmed
from memory.

Then without words,
distance shrinks
between two grown sisters,
separated halves,
any differences forgotten,
as their reaching arms touch.

Dancing Fountain

Random renditions
of complex water jets,
height,
duration,
erupt in
symphonic patterns
from a street level fountain
into the penetrating heat
of the town square.

Smiling children taken
by unpredictable rhythms
of ever changing streams
rush through a gap
in the broken curtain of water,
shoulders drawn,
arms lifted,
smiles dissolving into laughter—
Repeat, then repeat,
wet clothes pasted to skin.

Fewer more prudent adults,
beckoned
by the soul of the fountain,
plan their course
between the chords
of a liquid melody.
Gleefully they dart through
with measured precision,
just once, maybe twice,
helpless to outsmart the dance,
unwilling to soak themselves
before enchanted onlookers.

Unconcerned,
this intricate orchestra
continues bursting skyward.

Sleep

A hot shower of relief penetrates.
The edges of leaves or horses soften
as consciousness slips.
One becomes another, then back again.

The reds become blues,
blues become yellows become greens.
They erupt just shy of pain,
clear to the edges of visibility.

Time, space, and texture subside
into a swirling mass of water.
Any sound pierces perception
like a pin prick.

Gravity cradles the weight of fatigue.
Then gentle sleep, with elegant wings,
converges to begin its quiet renewal.
Like a silent melody, it wraps me in song.

Oatmeal Adventure

His smile breaks into stormy folds
as he bats away the oatmealed spoon
in his mother's hand.
His hard plastic bib complete with trough
lurches to one side,
spilling orphaned sticky oats
onto his chubby arm.

Spoon hijacked,
he wraps a determined fist
around it globe side up.
He stabs a single oat,
lifts the spoon
and pastes the morsel
onto his chin,
slides the spoon into his mouth,
stem sticking out,
eyes sparkling.
Mmmm he says waving his hands.

He digs in his dish for another oat.
It falls into his trough on the way
to his open mouth.
He picks up the gluey lump
and tosses it with a laugh
as his nerve endings reprogram
for heightened skill tomorrow.

Bright Boy

The small t-shirt on his even smaller torso
says *Look at the Bright Side.*
Cocked to one side like a beret
rests a blue bicycle helmet.
He sits on top of a yellow truck,
feet pushing to move him forward
until a large step looms.
He stands,
legs on either side of the truck
and lifts.
Then looks around.
Lifts and looks around.
Lifts and looks around.
He swings one leg over the truck,
pulls down his shorts,
squats, and pees a child size puddle.

A man offers help to lift the truck,
but bright boy pushes him away.
He wipes his hands
across the front of his t-shirt.
Then with shiny eyes
hoists the truck at last
up the imposing step.
A silent fanfare rises inside.
How comfortably his t-shirt
sits upon his chest
while his blue helmet protects
the bright side of fresh sensibility.

Murky Sunlight

Shadows fail to cast
their crisp silhouettes
in murky sunlight,
too wounded
to cut clean edges,
too fragile
to overcome ash
as a faraway fire
feeds its voracious appetite.

A Piano Falls

As I climb up a third flight of stairs,
a piano falls from the sky.
Invisible, silent.
It lands slowly, deliberately
burrowing into my quads.
No path to climb out.

Somewhere along the way
a neuron shifts.
A familiar handle sits just out of reach.
A window seems harder to open.
A distance stretches longer than expected.
A lock inadvertently catches.

Larger than before,
these skeletons wiggle
their nascent urgency
into the pathways
before me.

Moving Day

On moving day
the hard animal in my body
falls blindly into line
to burrow into the depths
of muscle fibers
ready to separate
these hundred boxes
one at a time
from the years of gravity
that cradles them
in a bed of inertia.

No thought for
lifting with my legs
or certainty of grip,
only shoving, removing, completing
as sweat drips
while myoglobin saturates
with lactic acid.

For days assaulted muscles
resent the effort spent
sending barbed echoes
into the soft recesses
of every limb,
the hard animal now reduced
to licking its wounds.

Spectator

Who is this alien asleep inside
that leaps awake when muscles flex
so a leather ball sails or almost sails
into a goal?

For a single infinite moment
it eclipses the sun,
our essence flying skyward
like a speeding asteroid
in the apex of motion
then landing once more,
spent, inside our core.

No matter that all the while
grass still grows,
arms push through sleeves,
daylight comes and goes.

Emptier than Empty

Handel's Messiah
swells in my living room.
Colored globes
glisten from my tree.
Christmas blooms
like daffodils in spring,
but still emptiness
like a tumor grows.

From an old LP,
the gentle strains of The First Noel
flood my mother's living room.
Paper hearts with m&m's inside
hung from her tree.
The green tablecloth with a red felt bow
made with her own hand.
Rhymes she wrote
on green and red packages
when fingers were nimble
and cognition was keen.

From thousands of miles away
my persistent recollections
mingle with Handel
in an empty stillness
while a family who never knew
my mother
inhabits her house.
The bench in her name
is all that's left,
anchored across the street
in the park
that shepherds a faded past.

Night Siren

The too near wail of an ambulance
assaults the quiet core of night,
its rising then falling crescendo
repeating, repeating,
unsettling all that is settled
as it announces
an unidentified human incident
rife with pain or loss or both.

Yet this ambulance,
defying disruption and speed limits,
delivers with singular purpose
a medical team
eager to serve, to make whole,
to mend the punctures of sharp protrusions
or the malfunction of a dusty heart
and to begin a restitution
that even in darkness has possibility.

Pfeiffer Canyon Bridge

Soggy ground shifts.
Rain follows more rain.
A pillar groans
as its footing slips
under the weight of a dying bridge.
Cracks travel up its spine
stealing life as they go.
The roadway sags.
Steel rebar peeks out of gaps.
Traffic ceases on a surface
too broken-hearted to connect
the sides of a yawning canyon.

Workers in hard hats and orange vests
with their jackhammer and iron ball
breathe the last life out of
the failing structure
as food, diesel fuel,
and homework from the school
travel by helicopter
across the gap.

With scraps of concrete
hoisted from their grave,
a trail pushes through,
an artery of life
with steps and bends
to feed the gaping canyon
until the new bridge is done.
Residents who knew only
their windshields
now exchange greetings
while walking to buy milk.

During their walk,
pounds dissolve into firmer flesh,
smokers quit their habit,
birds' songs reach thirsty ears,
and friendships begin.

Tight Braids

She sits on the edge of a bench in a red dress.
She rubs the back of her mostly fisted hands
back and forth on her thighs,
twists her arms,
tries to slide off the bench
as her mother from behind
steers her blond hair tightly into braids.

"Ow" she gasps pulling her head away.
The mother yanks on a braid
to bring the head back
as a single tear slides down the girl's face,
red as her dress,
and absorbs darkly into the fabric.

"No time for tears. Off we go" says the mother
who lets a braid fall from a grasp
that fails to open for the girl's hand,
rather picks up keys as eyes turn toward her car.

With every hair securely included in a braid
and feet in hard leather shoes
able to make loud noise on the pavement,
she stamps her feet recklessly
then hurries unhurriedly to shorten the distance
between herself and her mother's back.

Bicycle Chain

When running as it should,
dirt from miles around
hops on for the exalting ride.
Those little overlapping plates
their black beards
hugging pins at their junctures
travel round a spinning Ferris Wheel
serving an expedient pair of feet.
A thousand moving parts
squalidly pressing and squeezing
precisely against one another
to give birth to the motion
that feeds on a clean blue horizon.

We Can't Replant

Were the loss a favorite book
with a spine cracked
so yellowed pages lose their grip,
or a beloved sweater pilled
from tender friction
against the perimeters of things,
we could stay fastened to roots,
deep,
but not so deep
we can't replant.

While spread within the borders
of books and sweaters,
a broader resonance beckons
where blood and breath
and winsome ways
take hold our fictile hearts.

Brimming love
these captured hearts
endorse a higher calling
where love persists
as the loved perishes
and roots detach
beneath the weight of emptiness.
Here we can't replant.

The San Gabriel Aquaduct

Among a tangle of
ramshackle horse stables,
sprawling water reclamation plants,
towers strung with high tension wires,
and the overflow from auto lots,
lie the remains of the San Gabriel River
confined to a cavernous concrete canyon,
thief to cuckoos, brush rabbits, beetles,
and anadromous fish.

Complete with hydraulic dams,
rusting grocery carts,
and splintered plastic bottles
a thirty-eight mile aquaduct,
graveyard
to a diverse riparian habitat,
waits with a meager river
for a spine
to defuse the next flood.

Still this harnessed river,
its gold greedily pilfered away,
its flow altered for protection,
its aggregate mined for profit,
its life blood diverted for urban use
offers a venue
for an eclectic suburban playground
where cyclists sport their lycra,
families feast on carnitas,
and youngsters chase soccer balls.

Politeness

Politeness sweetens the pot of ourselves.
We spread it evenly on strangers
in a doorway or elsewhere,
a palatable carapace free from
demands or complexities.

But back it scales when familiarity
frays the threads of decorum
and swallows us whole.
In its place a cotyledon grows
bearing the seeds of hopeful mornings
side by side
with things we said or should have said.

Does sweetness ripen at last
or does it disintegrate
amidst proximity's friction?
Either way,
politeness serves as catalyst.

Banana Spots

The crackling green of early life
becomes the yellow jacket of pride
in perfect banana ripeness.
But soon shy specs of brown
rear their tiny heads,
grow confident,
mature into warrior spots
puffing out their chests,
charging into a softening yellow marsh,
rejoicing in their twilight advance.
Multiplying,
conquering,
until finally they join hands
and cover in a flaccid dusk
any lingering vestiges of ripeness.

Lunar Majesty

A waning crescent of the moon
grows thinner each night
as though it could buckle
under the gestating darkness
cradled to her breast.

But a single gold shaving
cast from this celestial body
holds firm like a mother's love
while the oceans of the earth
bow graciously, wordlessly
to her lunar majesty.

Yet as her waxing crescent
pushes into a shrinking shadow,
one with the night sky,
she plays tenderly with the light,
her edges soft and unpretentious,
hardly regal in their journey.

Marianne Brems has an MA in Creative Writing from San Francisco State University. She is a long time writer of nonfiction and her publications include textbooks in her teaching area of English as a Second Language and several trade books. She began writing poetry in mid life to capture essence and order in random events of daily life. She has a special interest in writing poems that exhibit a strong sense of transformation. Her poems have appeared in several literary journals including *The Pangolin Review, Armarolla, Foliate Oak, The Voice of Eve, La Scrittrice,* and *The Sunlight Press*. She lives in Northern California. Website: www.mariannebrems.com

www.ingramcontent.com/pod-product-compliance
Lightning Source LLC
LaVergne TN
LVHW041517070426
835507LV00012B/1631